ADVENTURES
IN
SERVICE
TO
GOD

PARTICIPANT'S WORKBOOK
FOR THE MINISTRY OF HELPS

"The Harvest is great but the workers are few." —Luke 10:2

REV. LAWRENCE C. SPENCER

WESTBOW
PRESS®
A DIVISION OF THOMAS NELSON
& ZONDERVAN

WestBow Press books may be ordered through booksellers or by contacting:

WestBow Press
A Division of Thomas Nelson & Zondervan
1663 Liberty Drive
Bloomington, IN 47403
www.westbowpress.com
1 (866) 928-1240

ISBN: 978-1-5127-6277-8 (sc)
ISBN: 978-1-5127-6278-5 (e)

Print information available on the last page.

WestBow Press rev. date: 10/28/2016

CONTENTS

OVERVIEW OF THE HELPS MINISTRY

Wow! If you're not excited about what God is about to do in your life, you should be. For those who have been to Helps Training before, enjoy the review and join in the discussions. For those who are new, welcome to the world of foot washers and table servers.

This series of classes will help fulfill the obligation God gives pastors and others in the five-fold ministry in Ephesians 4:11–14. It will give you the foundation needed to do two things: minister to the needs of people in the local church, and be a better witness of Jesus Christ to a lost and dying world.

Materials Needed:

- Your Bible
- This workbook
- Copies of the Code of Conduct and Helps Worker Applications

The big gaps between entries are reserved for you to fill in answers or make notes. Starting next week, when you go home from class, you must study the next week's lesson and fill in the blanks or write down questions prior to coming to the next class. The first few minutes of each class will be in small group discussions, and each attendee must be familiar with the lessons in order to participate in the class discussions.

Look up the Bible scriptures noted in the next lesson, mark them in your Bible, and highlight or write in your notes so you can find them quickly during the classes.

The objectives of this first lesson are:

- To show you a ministry ordained by God to unburden overworked pastors.
- To light the way for you to get involved in the Body of Christ in a new and satisfying way. That ministry is, of course, the Ministry of Helps. It has been with us since there was a church; it just didn't have the formal "Helps" name.

Let's look at the Great Commission (Mark 16:15). We are to go out and preach the good news. We can only accomplish this by everyone doing his or her part.

Why do we need an organized Helps Ministry? Among the multitude of challenges that face a local pastor, two come quickly to mind.

- Pastors who feel that they do not have enough time to do what they feel is needed.
- Pastors have a burden for souls, and they seek to grow their churches by saving new people.

Acts 6 shows us that the ancient Church had the same challenges. It was even bringing strife to the local body at that time. What did they do, and what was the result?

What the apostles did was pick out people they knew to have_____ and who had received the

_____, and _____them to do

_____ so the apostles could minister the Word of God.

Acts 6:7 shows us the result of doing it God's way. Three big things happened.

- First, the "Word of God Increased"—more preaching and teaching occurred.
- Second, the church grew in numbers: "the disciples multiplied." Not only that, but God gave them a bonus.
- Third, many Jewish priests became obedient to the faith. Remember, in these days, Christianity was an offshoot of Judaism, not a separate body. Converting a rabbi was a big deal. Converting people, including Jewish people, is still a big deal today.

The point here is that in the first seven verses of Acts 6, the Word gives us our instructions. It shows us how to free up a pastor's time and how to grow the Church. So let's not reinvent the wheel. God has given us specific instructions in his "instruction manual," so let's take his exhortation to heart and do what He tells us should be done. We'll discuss the practical aspects of this later.

In Ephesians 4:11, the Word admonishes pastors and other ministers to

_____.

Thus, the purpose of the Helps Ministry is to further the preaching of the Gospel and the winning of new souls by delegating duties away from the pulpit and into the hands of the saints. Thus the person in a ministerial office as outlined in Ephesians 4:11 can get on with the appointed tasks. Similarly, the person serving in a lay ministerial office as outlined in Romans 12 can do the "work of the ministry." That work is the great commission and running a local church so the work can occur.

1 Corinthians 12:27–28. Let's look at some scriptural proof that Helps is divinely ordained to serve the church. Paul clearly places the table workers and the church staff in some important company with this passage.

In this passage of scripture, along with excerpts from Ephesians 4:11 and 1 Corinthians 12:7–11, are two new words:_____ and _____. The King James Version says *Helps* and *Governments*, A modern language Bible might say, "help each other, and work together."

Turn back to v:**12**. Three of the five ministerial gifts are cited, and three of nine gifts of the Holy Spirit are mentioned:

_____, _____, and _____, with evangelists and pastors omitted.

_____, _____, and _____, with wisdom, knowledge, faith, prophesy, discerning of spirits, and interpretation of tongues not mentioned.

Neither God nor Paul wasted words. There is a reason that workers and leaders (governments) are mentioned in the same breath as the ministers in the church and the gifts of the Holy Spirit. The only apparent one is to elevate the practical worker's importance to the same level as the full-time ministry and the gifts of the Holy Spirit. Jesus teaches extensively about not thinking of yourself as better than another because of your position (e.g., sitting at the special place at a table). Those of us who are workers in God's Church must be humble and serve the congregation as we would serve God Himself. Thus, this passage clearly seeks to place all of us on the same level.

There are three important Greek words used for *worker* in the New Testament. Two apply to lay workers, and the third applies to the ministry.

- Diakonos, or Deacon, is a server, a waiter on the flock, a table server. In Mark 10:43, Jesus said whoever wants to be great among you must be your servant.
- Huperetes, or under rower or seaman, later signifies anyone working under another. In Acts 26:16, it is used of Paul as a servant of Christ.
- The third word in common use was Leitourgos a public servant, a minister. It's used by Jesus in Hebrews 8:2 ("Minister of the Sanctuary"), and in Romans 15:16 Paul says "a minister of Christ Jesus." We get the term "Liturgical form of church government" from this word.

The first two, Diakonos and Huperetes, are the words used in 1 Corinthians 12:28—not the third one. The emphasis was on the saints of the Church becoming involved and doing the "work of the ministry." This work was as important as the ministerial gifts and the Holy Spirit gifts. There is no other logical or theological reason for this passage except to exhort us to greater works in God's service.

Our duties are clear. Winning converts to Christ by assisting our pastor in our area (our world) and ministering to the people. In Romans 16:1–16, Paul gives credit to many members of the Helps Ministry who assisted him in his missionary work. A fun exercise to do at home is to read these passages and substitute the names of your fellow workers in this church. It makes the Bible very personal, because it is. It is the same yesterday today and forever. Remember that Jesus is the Word. Wow, this is fun, isn't it?

Let's recap the important points so far.

Mark 16:15 is for who? _____

Acts 6 cites _____

Ephesians 4:11 _____

1 Corinthians 12 _____,

and in verse 28 He places workers in the same passage as the Holy Spirit gifts and the ministry gifts in Ephesians 4:11, and admonishes us to desire the greater gifts.

WHERE DO WE GET THE WORKERS?

Now we get to the practicalities of Acts 6 in the Word. It is safe to assume that in ancient times, the apostles knew most of the seventy intimately, including many others as very close associates. Jesus's ministry lasted only three years, and many were with him for a lot of that time. It follows that the apostles probably had a large number of people to choose from to get seven men full of the Spirit and wisdom to wait on the tables of the widows.

In our world, where people move around a lot and live farther apart, we have a harder time finding qualified workers. As leaders, we must use wisdom to seek out and train workers. This ministry training system with pastors and leaders in the discussion groups is the way we have chosen to follow the biblical mandate "to seek out people full of the spirit and wisdom" in order to put in helps jobs in the local church.

Let's make a list of attributes we are looking for.

- Born again and says so.
- Baptized in the Holy Spirit and has the evidence of speaking in tongues. (Note: we can accomplish this in the training program.)
- Has a trainable spirit, not argumentative; wise.
- Obedient, a tither.
- Faithful in attendance.
- Willing to make a time commitment of twelve weeks of training and six months of service.
- Demonstrates a Christian lifestyle (1 Timothy 3).
- Signs and lives up to the code of conduct while in the Helps Ministry.

Beware of making your list too long. We are looking for people with the right attitude, not perfection. This list of attributes was made up by a local church. It is set up by the local church. Remember, where Bible is concerned, a rule is _____. Where local custom is concerned, it is _____ as we need it to be here in the local church.

Recruits would include anyone aspiring to full-time ministry. The Helps Ministry is wonderful training in church organization, with less responsibility than people will have as full-time ministers. It's a great training ground for future pastors.

Anyone in Bible school should spend significant time in a Helps capacity; this will demonstrate faithfulness to a local body. Also, the pastor and others supervising their education can judge the "fruits of their ministry."

For regular members of the congregation, it offers a sense of belonging. For adults, it is a way of mentoring the younger generation. For the youth, it is a great way to take on responsibility in a structured way and learn skills needed in adulthood.

Training

This training course is the beginning. You are being trained as a present or future leader in this local body. It is the pastor's responsibility to know you have a certain level of knowledge as you minister to the flock God has assigned to him. He is fulfilling his duty by creating this program to standardize the training locally so it complies with the Word of God and the pastor's vision for the church.

Those of you who are presently in ministry or are selected for ministry will learn how to organize and supervise a function and train your replacement or stand-in. Many of you may have experience in ministry; few have had formal training in how to run one. None know how a local pastor wants to operate until that pastor instructs them. This program was created to be taught by the pastor and those in leadership. As you complete the training, some of you will become instructors. This is how Jesus ran his ministry, instructing the disciples, the seventy, and others and admonishing them that greater things will they do in his name than even He did. Your pastor is sponsoring this program to instruct you in the skills needed to win souls, and then he or she will send you out to do just that.

Whether you are a musician, usher, nursery worker, or yard maintainer, you have the great commission, and your pastor has the responsibility to get you doing the "work of the ministry." May God bless your studies, and may you faithfully complete them and obtain your certificate of completion.

One task that you will learn late in the instruction is how to plan and organize a ministry. Use this manual and remember the admonishment in the New Living Translation of Proverbs 24:3–4. I will read it, so please copy it into your manual. It will help you remember an important Bible truth that can help you in ministry and in life in general.

_____

_____

_____

The three key words in this passage are wisdom, common sense, and knowledge (keeping abreast of the facts). If we approach life and our ministries remembering this, we will be more successful.

We exist to fulfill the great commission. We must be wise in our use of tangible and human resources to be the most effective. These classes will begin to prepare you to truly minister to God's Church. The Helps Ministry is a win-win proposition for everyone. It's biblical, it's practical, and it's fun.

Next week, we start the code of conduct. Read it in your workbook, and remember it is for workers only. You do not have to adhere to any code of conduct to merely attend the church. It is not a secret document, but it is not for general sharing with church members. Someone may make the mistake of thinking it is required of members or people who attend our church. No! Only workers who voluntarily sign the code of conduct must follow it.

Please read ahead in lesson 2 and place bookmarks at the Bible scriptures listed in the lesson. There are a lot of them. Your other reading assignment is to read 1 Timothy 3. It will only take a few minutes, and it will give you an appreciation for how an overseer (Paul) and your pastor feel and think about someone who is going to minister under them. Pretend the letter is written to you instead of Timothy. It may not all apply to you, but pray that God will reveal to you, through the Holy Spirit, what He wants you to get out of that reading. We will discuss the code of conduct next week.

LESSON 2

SETTING THE EXAMPLE

I used 1 Timothy 3 as the inspiration for this formal code of conduct. Remember, this code of conduct is for workers, paid staff, and leaders only.

We hope that as we live up to the code, our example as leaders will lead the congregation to a better lifestyle in Christ. However, as a local church, we can only require compliance with a formal written code from committed workers, paid staff, and Bible students. Only these people who have signed the code of conduct will be required to live by it.

This code is not for distribution to the members of the congregation. They might become confused and mistakenly think they have to comply in order to be members or attendees of the church. This is not the case, as you know. We welcome all in our church regardless of their current lifestyles. Our charge is to reconcile them with Jesus Christ and to love them into fellowship with God. We should not judge them by the code of conduct to which we subject ourselves.

The code of conduct in the manual stays there for your reference. The instructor will give you a single page copy to sign for the church's record.

The following text of the code of conduct has extra space for comments, questions you might want to ask, or concerns you may have. We will be discussing each item in the small-group discussions next week. However, please feel free to consult with the instructor or make an appointment with the pastor if you have any question or concern about this, or about any other topic in the Helps Training Program.

This is the "instruction version" of the code of Conduct. The actual code is one page long and only highlights some of the text found here in the workbook.

To speak in one accord with the leadership of this church (1 Corinthians 1:10), the congregation must see all of us supporting the pastor and enthusiastically pursuing his vision for the local congregation. Any differences of opinion are to be discussed in Helps Ministry Training classes like this one, or privately with the person involved (Matthew 18:15–17).

To Live a Clean Life (1 Corinthians 6:19–20). I will not defile the temple of God (my body) with smoking, drinking alcoholic beverages, using illicit drugs, immoral sex, or other unhealthy practices. This should be a no-brainer, but many think that it is okay to indulge in these things as long as you love Jesus. You may be a work in progress, and some in the church may drink and smoke. But if you are going to be in Helps, you cannot.

1 Timothy 3:2. As an example of self-control and respectability, I will keep myself clean of body and breath, and I'll dress in clean and appropriate clothes as a living example of how Jesus would have me look as His representative on earth. We are His only witnesses. How we look, smell, and conduct ourselves is how He is judged by the unsaved and the new baby Christians. This item is all about example.

Matthew 24:45-46. I will faithfully be on time to and attend all church services when I am scheduled to work. I will never miss a function where I am scheduled to work without getting a substitute. (Emergencies are excepted—for example, an accident on the way to church.) It would be nice if all workers made every activity. But remember your priorities. You cannot ignore time with God, family, or your employment simply to have a perfect attendance record at church.

I will be reliable and dependable on my assigned job (Proverbs 18:9). Further, when I sign up, I will be there to work. It is much better to not sign up than to lead the pastor to believe a job will be done but not show up (Proverbs 12:17). Remember that in this church, we make six-month commitments. At the end of six months, you are released unless you decide to reenlist. If the job is not for you, then you can try another, or you can rest in the congregation and then enlist again when time permits.

This next point follows #5. I agree to tell my supervisor if I am being used too much. I will not wait until burnout occurs and then quit in anger (Matthew 18:15).

I will complete all training even if I have heard it before (Proverbs 13:16; 15:5; 15:32; 19:20). Please keep an open mind and a trainable attitude.

I agree to make myself available as an exhorter if needed, even if my job is behind the scenes and not with people. Jesus gave us all the great commission to preach the Gospel, and I must be instant in season to be able to witness salvation, healing, baptism in the Holy Spirit, and deliverance. If the pastor or other leader calls, I agree to serve as an exhorter or usher, or any other job at any time I am needed during a service.

I agree to tithe the first 10 percent of my finances and of my time to God. I will take time to diligently pray for my family, my church, my country, my secular job, and all mankind (Hebrews 7:1–10; Malachi 3:8–11). Under the New Covenant, we can tithe more than 10 percent. People who aspire to the Helps Ministry must be tithers. We would like everyone to tithe into this body to further the work locally, but we do not check. However, when you put in your application, we will check to make sure you are a regular giver.

I agree to obey the leadership without question during any organized service. The Holy Spirit places leaders in place. An organized service is an inappropriate place to question authority or anointing. Save your questions or suggestions for training sessions or at a time other than at an organized service (Titus 3:1).

I agree to take the time to get "prayed up" prior to going on my job, so I can be operating supernaturally in the will of God on my Helps job. This is also a good practice for your secular job. When worldly things happen that make you uncomfortable, the Holy Spirit can bring "all things to remembrance" to help you through the difficult time (John 14:26).

As a favor to my pastor, I agree to accept temporary assignment in another job to fill a need until someone else is found. This should seldom happen. Three weeks will be the limit of substitutions, not the normal six-month commitment.

I agree to keep my children under control as an example to other parents, and so that mine don't lead others astray (1 Timothy 3:4).

I will faithfully live and study the Word of God to the best of my ability. I'll show myself as approved, so I can be an example of prosperity and great success (2 Timothy 2:15; Joshua 1:8).

BORN AGAIN: A FREE GIFT FROM GOD

This is the first of four foundational lessons in the Helps Ministry training program. Next week you will be expected to know the information in this lesson and be prepared to discuss it in class. The objective is to get you comfortable in winning souls to Christ. A lively class discussion and practical application of the information in the lesson cannot occur unless you do your part in preparation. This lesson is comprised of information found on a fairly long tract entitled "Born Again."

START TRACT

The words "born again" have been misunderstood for many years. Religious people sometimes feel that it only applies to "low brow" people—you know, the ones who don't have a good academic understanding of what church is about. They may confine the term to what Baptists or Holy Roller Pentecostals believe. Others consider it a term made popular by evangelists on radio and TV. These and all other non-biblical explanations are wrong!

Born again is not a term invented by any religion or denomination. Jesus himself coined the phrase in John 3:1–21.

In the Bible, a Jewish religious leader who was highly respected in the community came to Jesus and commented on the miracles Jesus was performing. Jesus did not acknowledge his words. Instead, Jesus replied, "Unless you are born again you cannot see the Kingdom of God." Nicodemus was that religious man. He then started discussing the born again subject with Jesus. Perhaps he was trying to understand in his mind, in his senses, what being born again was all about.

Today, many people are still missing the point of Jesus's message: that you must believe by faith, not making up your mind or reasoning things out. This is a blessing God has provided for us. Jesus told Nicodemus that you are born once from your mother's womb, which is the physical birth (born of water). However, being born again is a personal, spiritual choice you make to believe in Jesus Christ as your Lord and Savior.

Jesus explains this in John 3:16 and John 3:36, and Paul elaborates on the choice in Romans 10:9–17. Read these and make them a part of yourself. In 2 Corinthians 5:17, the Bible tells us that if anyone (and anyone includes you who are reading this now) is in Christ, he or she becomes a new creature. This means that the old us—the sinner, the failure, the dissatisfied part of us—is passed away. In Jesus we become new spirits. We are spirit men, and we have a soul (mind, emotions, and intellect). The Spirit is renewed, and the body and mind are ours to renew and improve.

Jesus was brutally beaten and then crucified on the cross. He shed his blood for your sins. He went to hell and defeated Satan for you! Then he was raised from the dead by God, preached for a while, and went up to heaven to be with God. He sits at the right hand of the Father now, preparing a place for you up there. He is reaching out to you now through these words and through the person who gave you this tract.

You receive the new birth by faith, through the grace of God. You cannot earn it through religious service, teaching Sunday school, doing good works, being honest, or even through the intercession of a member of the clergy. Look at Ephesians 2:8–10. You'll see that the good works are the result of being born again, not a requirement ahead of time.

You will find that being born again is a free gift from God. Sometimes at sports gatherings you see a banner that says, "**John 3:16**." That verse states, "God so loved the world [including you and I[that He gave his only Son [Jesus] so that anyone [not just the good people, but *anyone*] who believes in Him will not perish but will have eternal life [with Jesus in heaven]." Wow!

You can have it too! You can receive Jesus Christ as your personal savior right now. You can have eternal life for yourself in heaven. You can also begin to learn His promises for the abundant and healthy life He has for you on this earth now. Pray the prayer of salvation right now. Pray out loud. Do it now—don't delay another minute. Say this prayer to God, believe it in your heart, and speak it with your lips.

Dear God, I believe that Jesus Christ is Lord and that he was born as a man, was crucified for me, died and went to hell, and defeated the devil for me. God, you raised him from the dead, and now He is sitting in heaven at Your right hand. I confess Jesus as my personal Lord and Savior. I confess my sins and repent of them, and I know that You are faithful to forgive me of all my sins. I receive my forgiveness by faith and thank You that I am now born again, a new person in Jesus Christ. In His name I pray, amen,

Praise God. You did it—you just became a born-again believer! You are a new creature in Jesus Christ not because you look or feel like it, but because God says so. Now that you are a new Christian, you have all the rights and promises contained in the Bible. You also take on all the responsibilities of a Christian. You will always have the freedom of choice: you can do it God's way or your way. In Romans 12:2, the Bible admonishes us to renew our (intellectual) minds.

A good start is by getting a Bible and reading it to discover what God has to say about how to live your life. Remember, the Bible is the only infallible reference for how we are to live our lives. Reject the worship, or holding in reverence, or practice of any tradition or teaching that does not line up with the Word of God.

Also, change what you put into your mind every day. Read things about your occupation, your health, and some Christ-centered literature (Christian bookstores have a lot of it). Changing what you feed your mind will help make you the better person you want to be. You will become a new person outwardly as well as spiritually. Strive to be better on the job as a worker or supervisor, and be better at home as a parent or child. And most of all, be better equipped to pass on this great gift of salvation to another person.

Be better, and when people wonder why, you then have a chance to tell them what happened to you. Tell them about the Jesus who saved you and can save them too! In 2 Timothy 2:15, Paul sends a strong message to Timothy to "Study to show himself approved." That same message is good for us today.

Next, share this tract with someone new. Give them a chance to know Jesus too. In Mark 16:15, Jesus tells us to go out into the world and preach the Gospel to every creature. You may only know what is in this tract and what has happened to you, but you can witness (preach) what you know to another person. You can help them build their faith and accept Jesus Christ as their personal Lord and Savior. You can do it, and God will bless your efforts.

Finally, join a church that openly and joyfully preaches the uncompromised Word of God. Many churches water down the Word: they say that miracles are not for today, or they may mix the Bible with some other sacred book or denominational teaching. Some may have some man or group of men have revelation not contained in the Bible, and you have to obey their teachings.

In Galatians 1:8, Paul deals with churches, denominations, people, and even angels who use things outside of Bible to set religious doctrine. "But even if we or an angel from heaven, preach any other gospel to you than what we have preached, let him be accursed." Wow—strong words.

Remember, it is the words that are preached and the precepts that are taught which are important. Denominational labels are not important. Listen to the preacher, make an appointment, and meet with him or her. If you are met with discouragement, or if people say something is "not for today," then leave that place immediately.

Pray for God's Holy Spirit to reveal to you where you should worship. Your spiritual life depends on the food (the teachings) the man or woman of God feeds you. Choose carefully, take notes, and then go home and check the notes with the Word of God. If that is the right place for you, then *join*, become a diligent worker, tithe honestly and faithfully, God will bless your obedience to His Word.

END OF TRACT

Next week, we review baptism in the Holy Spirit. Read your lesson ahead of time. Most of us have heard many sermons on this topic and have seen people get baptized. The purpose of this next lesson is to get all of us comfortable with praying someone through the baptism. Don't be just a watcher, but a doer of the Word. If you don't have the baptism in the Holy Spirit, you can get it next week!

Assignment for this week: Along with reading the Bible scriptures for next week, seek out someone you know who wants the baptism in the Holy Spirit. Bring them to class with you. Tell them you have a written guarantee that they will get the baptism in the Holy Spirit at the class if they earnestly want it.

Guarantee: You have your pastor's permission to read 1 Corinthians 12:7 and Luke 11:13 to anyone who wants to hear them!

LESSON 4

BAPTISM IN THE HOLY SPIRIT

This lesson is the second in the training of workers to be exhorters of the Word of God. Many new people are eager to receive salvation—that's pretty standard in the Christian tradition. Believing in Jesus and confessing him as our Savior is fairly universal over the Christian denominations. It's called by different names, but it is acceptable. Baptism in the Holy Spirit does not enjoy this widespread acceptance. There are denominations that will expel you if they find out you are baptized in the Holy Spirit. Others ignore the parts of the Bible that teach on the "charismatic gifts"

Witnessing to new converts about baptism in the Holy Spirit could be resisted because of false teachings they have had or prejudices they may harbor. We must therefore be mindful of Paul's teaching in 1 Corinthians 1:1–3. We must approach the new convert or the person who resists the teaching with love.

The first recipients of the baptism in the Holy Spirit were given the promise and told by Jesus, after the resurrection, to stay in Jerusalem; in a few days, they would will be baptized with the Holy Spirit. This instruction tells us that Jesus was giving his people choice. If they chose not to stay, they could go on as they were, and go to heaven. But if they chose to stay, and if they earnestly desired the baptism in the Holy Spirit, they would be "clothed with power from on high" (Luke 24:49).

In John 16:5, Jesus goes into detail in promising the Holy Spirit, the Counselor, the Spirit of Truth to give the disciples power to do the work of bringing people to Jesus. Check out verse 8: "when he [the Holy Spirit] comes, he will convict the world of guilt in regard to sin and righteousness and judgment."

In Luke 11:13, Jesus promises the Holy Spirit to anyone who asks. This is a key scripture, because it's Jesus making a promise to everyone today, and He did it over two thousand years ago. Hebrews 13:8 says Jesus is the same yesterday, today, and forever. His testimony is truth and life. Therefore when we witness to folks to aid them in receiving baptism in the Holy Spirit, it is important to remember these scriptures, especially if you don't have a tract handy.

Remember that the Word works! We may have great opinions and interesting experiences to impart, but everything we have is weak when compared with the power of the Living Word of God—your Bible.

Let's go to a tract. In a few minutes, we will get some people up front and have receivers and prayers. The receivers will get the baptism in the Holy Spirit, and hopefully we have some people in the group who earnestly desire the baptism—people who are obedient Christians and who love Jesus. Born-again Christians who desire the power Jesus promised more than anything. If so, you can receive it from Jesus here tonight.

If we don't have anyone needing the baptism, then we need some volunteers to be the receivers. Instead of getting it for the first time, you can get another in filling of Jesus's power and become an even more effective witness.

Before we start, we need to go over the first part of the tract. If you are praying with someone after a service, you need to find out where they are in the Word. How much of the altar call preaching do they remember? The first few paragraphs of the tract are instructional and help them to understand the baptism. The paragraphs after the prayer give them more understanding as to what happened and what they can expect.

I'll read the first portion, and then we will bring the folks up front. You will receive the Holy Spirit baptism now. When you come up, expect to receive it—this is not pretend. We don't play Bible. This is going to be one of the most memorable times of someone's life in a few minutes. Thank You, Jesus, for sending us the Holy Spirit.

START TRACT

Baptism in the Holy Spirit: A Gift That Is for Today!

> There are over six hundred references to the Spirit in the Bible. He is the third person of the Trinity: Father God, Jesus God, and God the Holy Spirit. Many of these references refer to the Holy Spirit and the power He gives to people. This short study will start with John the Baptist's prophesy of a baptism in the Holy Spirit which the Messiah will bring.

This is promised in all four Gospels (Matthew 3:11; Mark 1:8; Luke 3:16; John 1:33) and at least twenty other places in the New Testament. John's prophesy carry much authority because Jesus described him by saying, "There is not a greater prophet than John The Baptist" (Luke 7:26–28).

After His resurrection, Jesus again promised the Holy Spirit. At Pentecost, 120 people including Mary (Jesus's earthly mother), and his brothers received baptism in the Holy Spirit. Further, they began to speak in unknown tongues! It must have sounded weird, like a lot of adults babbling baby talk. The Bible tells us that many foreign visitors in Jerusalem heard this babbling as their own native tongue! Others who did not speak these languages heard it and thought the 120 were drunk on wine. Of the people who heard it in their own language, many got saved. Acts chapter 2 gives us the history of this first day. After the original 120 received baptism, others received it by faith quickly, when prayed with by one of the Spirit-baptized people.

The people who judged the situation in worldly terms probably still thought they were drunk or a bunch of fanatics. In Acts 2:40–41 we see that Peter pleaded with people to repent, suggesting that some did not heed his pleading. Verse 42 states, "those who accepted," indicating some did not accept Jesus, get saved, or get baptized in the Holy Spirit.

Make sure your candidates have accepted Jesus, has repented of their sins, and want to live as testimony to Jesus. No one is perfect, but make sure people really are sincere. Remember verse 41: "Those who accepted." There is no faking baptism in the Holy Spirit. If you earnestly want it, Jesus promises it to us, and you will receive.

The setting of praying with someone could be after an altar call where a group prayer was offered for the baptism, or in a personal setting, or anywhere you find a person desiring the gifts. We need to be ready to assist no matter what our church function is.

There are nine gifts of the Holy Spirit given by Jesus for us to do the work He set out for us to do. We received the right to receive the gifts when we accepted salvation. However, being immersed or baptized in the Holy Spirit is a separate act of grace. Jesus promised the gift to us. It is ours today if we earnestly seek the Holy Spirit and obediently follow Jesus.

Usually we do not receive the baptism when we receive salvation because the person who prayed with us for salvation only told us enough of the Word to get us to the place we could believe in Jesus and accept Him as our personal Savior. Not hearing the Word of God concerning the baptism equals no knowledge that the gift exists, and usually this equals not getting the baptism. There are people who get saved and baptized in the Holy Spirit from reading a tract like this one. Praise God; we hope you will too. But most often it's a Christian who teaches you about the gifts and prays with you until you receive the gifts.

Faith (for salvation, for baptism in the Holy Spirit, or for anything else) comes by hearing and understanding God's Word, the Bible (Romans 10:17). If there is no preaching about the Holy Spirit, the result is people will not learn about or receive the baptism in the Holy Spirit. This tract is to make up for preaching you never heard or that you did not understand. Take this information and believe with all your heart that Jesus will baptize you in the Holy Spirit, and He will. You need to be obedient to, hunger for, and believe you will receive it. You do your part, and He will do His part.

Speaking in tongues is the initial outward sign that you have received the baptism in the Holy Spirit. Much of this tract is devoted to that topic. The other gifts are for your further Bible study or another class later on. Like on the day of Pentecost, when some judged tongues harshly and criticized the Christians, it still goes on today. There are sincere Christians who misinterpret the Bible and believe that tongues are not for today—or worse, are of the devil!

However, the Bible tells us that Jesus is the same yesterday, today, and forever (Hebrews 13:8). Jesus is still baptizing people in the Holy Spirit, and we are still speaking in tongues! Nothing has changed. Christians are still operating in the supernatural gifts of the Holy Spirit, and we are still being judged by religious people. Follow Jesus and believe what God says through the Bible, not what man says.

All the gifts of the Spirit revealed to us in 1 Corinthians 12–14 are for us today. We will continue to need and rely upon these gifts until the revelation of God's will is perfect and the Gospel is complete. We look to Revelation chapter 21, where God's Bible tells us that the final perfection is when God dwells with us and we with him. Obviously there will be no need for spiritual gifts then, because He will be with us.

Until that time, Jesus's great commission given to us in Mark 16:15–20 is still in operation. We must be obedient to Jesus's instructions to go out in the world and tell everyone about Him. The Holy Spirit is the enabler, through the spiritual gifts, for us to be more effective witnesses of Jesus Christ. We obediently do the job He told us to do, using the gift he promised us to enable us to be good witnesses. The Gospel is complete when Jesus returns, not before.

Baptism in the Holy Spirit, like salvation, is a gift that is promised to us by God. He doesn't give any bad gifts; He loves us too much. You can receive baptism in the Holy Spirit right now! Jesus said in Luke 11:13 that God will give the Holy Spirit to them that ask Him. *Them* means anyone, and that means you and any anyone else who earnestly seeks the gift and asks Jesus sincerely for the gifts. He will baptize you in the Holy Spirit.

Pray this prayer out loud to God. Believe in faith that He will baptize you in the Holy Spirit, and that you will speak in an unknown tongue.

> Dear God, I come to you as a born-again believer in Jesus Christ. I believe that you raised Him from the dead and He is in Heaven with you now. I confess Him as my Lord and Savior. Now I ask for baptism in the Holy Spirit. I declare to You that I will receive it in faith and use my mouth to speak in a tongue that I cannot understand.
>
> In Jesus's name, I cast out any spirit of fear, unbelief, prejudice, or embarrassment that would try to hinder me. I replace it with a spirit of faith in Your promise to give me the baptism in the Holy Spirit if I asked you for it. So, right now, in Jesus's name, I receive by faith the baptism in the Holy Spirit.

Now that you have been baptized in the Holy Spirit, whether you are alone or praying with someone, close your eyes, praise God, and thank Him for baptizing you. God inhabits the praise of his children. Continue praising Him. Now, begin to praise Him and thank Him in a language you have never spoken. Control your tongue and make words in faith, in a language you do not know. Do it in faith; you have to move the tongue and lips, you have to talk, and you have say something in faith.

What you are doing here is described in 1 Corinthians 14:15, praying to God in your own understanding (your native language) and praying to Him in the Spirit (or a language you do not know, also called your prayer language). What you are doing is entirely biblical. Praise him in faith. Later on, in your private prayer time, start praising him often in tongues daily for five minutes or so. Make it a sacrifice of praise to God for blessing you with salvation and baptism in the Holy Spirit.

There are four types of tongues revealed to us in the Word of God. (On the actual tract, they will be printed in the text. Here, they are blank so you can fill them in to help you remember them.)

First: _____ _____. See 1 Corinthians 14:2, 4, 14; Jude 20.

Second: Tongues _____, for exhortation, as a sign for the unbeliever. See 1 Corinthians 14:22, 26–28.

Third: Tongues as a_____

_____ This happened at Pentecost, when the visitors to Jerusalem heard the newly Spirit-baptized believers speaking in the listener's native language. See Acts 2:4–6.

Fourth: And _____. A manner of praying in situations where we are so overcome that we cannot think of the appropriate words. The Spirit gives utterance here, and we do not have control of what comes out of our mouths. See Romans 8:26.

God has provided tongues as a free gift. He expects you to use it for His glory. Some denominations and some people do not believe in tongues or any of the other gifts of the Holy Spirit mentioned in 1 Corinthians 12:8–10. Keep in mind that people's opinions, preferences, or prejudices do not nullify or modify the Word of God. God's Word (the Bible) is fact; man's interpretation of the Bible is frequently incorrect.

Some people fear that tongues or other of the gifts of the Spirit may be misused as they were in Corinth in Paul's time, so they don't teach about them. Others, out of incorrect teaching, ignorance, or tradition, feel that the gifts aren't real or are not for today. Please read the Bible. Believe what God says to you through the written Word. Believe what Jesus said He would do. Reject man's teaching to the contrary. Do not fear or reject the gifts that God wants to give you. Praise Him for all the gifts, and give each the reverence and respect that a God-given gift deserves.

Now, your next step is to let the Holy Spirit lead you to a local church where you can serve God, and where you can learn the Word and pass it on to others. This will enable you to do the job Jesus wants you to do: to tell the whole world about Jesus. If someone prayed with you to receive the baptism, ask the person for guidance. Or go to the church of your youth if you had one, or look in the phone book for a "full Gospel" church. That's a Christian code cord for a church that believes in the present-day gifts of the Holy Spirit.

END OF TRACT

Some people will receive a more enthusiastic outpouring of tongues than others. But all who earnestly ask will receive; Jesus said so, and that makes it fact. The next step is to encourage each person you pray with (or exhort about the baptism) to pray daily in tongues.

The newly baptized believer needs to develop confidence and faith and should speak out in tongues daily. Use the example of "confess with your mouth and believe in your heart that Jesus is Lord" (Romans 10:10). To evidence salvation, you need to confess Jesus is your Lord. To evidence baptism in the Holy Spirit, you need to speak in tongues. Both are acts of faith. Encourage others to pray in tongues in their private time, commune with God, and grow in Christ. Also encourage them to read the tract and look up the scriptures. Get them into the Word!

If they mention that they are in a church that opposes Spirit-filled people, you have a delicate issue to overcome. The Bible is your resource; quote it often, and don't criticize the denomination or the clergy that has an opposing opinion. Never criticize God's anointed. Simply repeat the Word, preach the Word, and let God and the Holy Spirit do the convicting and the convincing.

Lead them tenderly and lovingly to a place where they can be sensitive to the leading of the Spirit, and have Him lead them to the place where they should be. Avoid the temptation to get them immediately involved in your church. If they are totally unchurched and have no preference, then by all means bring them to your church. Move slowly and give support and comfort, but do not proselytize from another Christian Church.

To stay on track, people need fellowship with other Spirit-filled believers. Offer that support, but let the Spirit decide whether or not to move them from another church. He may have a work for them to do there. Don't play God.

Keep Galatians 1:8 in mind, and have the new believer underline it in their Bible. If anyone, even an angel, preaches a gospel different than what the apostles preached, let them be accursed. Those are strong words—words of condemnation. But the Bible said it not us. Newly baptized people are going to have to discover truth for themselves. They will learn that those who preach against baptism in the Holy Spirit, or against anything else that the apostles preached, is wrong. It is not for us to talk against another church or denomination. We just preach Jesus and Him risen.

Study lesson 5 for next week, and please read Deuteronomy 28.

HEALING

There are two absolutes that must be understood by every person taking this training. These two items are not negotiable or up for discussion. If you cannot adhere to these two rules, then please leave the program now.

All persons ministering under the auspices of this local church must know and obey these two rules without exception.

- *Never* is a person to be advised to stop seeing their doctor.
- *Never* is a person to be advised to stop taking medication that he is taking on advice of a doctor.

John 2:23. Many believed in Jesus because of the miracles he did. In John 14:11, Jesus asks us to believe in Him and claims He is God and God is in Him; believe for the works' (miracles') sake. Then read the scripture important to our studies in this lesson, verse 13, and whatsoever you ask in my name that will I do that the Father may be glorified in the Son. Keep going to verse 14: "If you ask anything in my name I will do it."

We are charged with praying for the sick in James 5:14. In 1 Peter 2:24 and Isaiah 53:5, the Bible tells us that Jesus bore our sins in his own body, and by his stripes we were healed.

In this introduction, we want to start building the confidence in you that you do have the right and the privilege to pray with the sick for healing. God has the responsibility to heal, not you. Let's go into this tract and begin our lesson. This tract was written so it could be used by a person who found it and had no Bible training. It can also be use as a reference for mature Christians as they witness to and pray for the sick.

REV. LAWRENCE C. SPENCER

START TRACT

Healing Is for Today

To be healed, believe in faith that what God says is truth all the time, every time. What life's experiences or religion teaches us may be false. What God says in the Bible is truth, and you need to believe in faith what God says about healing and health. You must reject both your life experience and religious teachings that are contrary to God's Word. Even stronger than that, by holding on to this unbelief you are in effect calling God a liar! When you reject God's Word, you also reject the blessings and promises contained in it.

Next, know where sickness came from. When Adam and Eve sinned against God and gave up the earth to Satan, sickness and death started. God explains this in Genesis chapter 3, when Adam and Eve lost the protection of God in the garden, and were driven out. The devil now had a "lease on the earth." Adam had given up the dominion God gave to him. To this day, Satan has dominion over the temporal earth.

In John 10:10, Jesus tells us that the devil comes to steal, kill, and destroy. It is apparent that he has done a great job these thousands of years! But praise God, for the second part of John 10:10 says that Jesus has come that we may have life, and life more abundantly. You don't have to have your health and happiness stolen; you need not be killed by disease. You are promised the abundant life by Jesus himself!

The Bible tells us that God is not a liar (Numbers 23:19, Titus 1:2, Hebrews 6:18). When He says that He is the God that Heals us (Exodus 15:26), that there has not failed one word of His good promise (1 Kings 8:56), and that He will hasten His Word to perform it (Jeremiah 1:12), this means that He is the God that heals us. He is not a liar, and He keeps His word! God is not a respecter of persons (Acts 10:34), and because He healed others at other times, He will heal you now! Psalms 119:89 says that "Forever Lord your Word is settled in Heaven." That means past, present, and future, forever.

Jesus taught us how to pray in Matthew 6:10. We call it the Lord's Prayer. Remember these words: "thy will be done on earth as it is in heaven." In 3 John 2, the Apostle John says, "Beloved [that's you and I], I wish above all things that you prosper and be in health even as your soul prospers."

Jesus himself bore our sicknesses when He was beaten before and during His crucifixion. First Peter 2:24 says by His stripes (beatings), we were healed, so it is already done! Believe the Bible, not what your experience, feelings, or religion teaches you if it does not line up with God's Word. If any statement, teaching, or belief is counter to God's Word, then it is wrong and should be rejected as a lie. Healing is for today and is for now; claim it in the name of Jesus. He wants you well.

In John 6:38 Jesus said, "I came down from Heaven not to mine own will, but in Him that sent me." The healing miracles that Jesus did were God's will in action. Nothing in the Bible suggests that God's will changed simply because Jesus and the original apostles are no longer in their mortal bodies. In Hebrews 13:8, we are told that Jesus is the same yesterday, today, and forever. Jesus himself ordered s believers to go out and preach the Gospel. Further, He tells us to lay hands on the sick, and they will recover. Did Jesus lie to us? Hardly. He never lied.

Read Mark 16:15–20. Jesus is talking to you here! Also read John Chapter 14 carefully. Here, Jesus specifically promises the Holy Spirit and power even greater than He had. Also, note our obligations.

If you have just been prayed for, or hands laid on you for healing, or if you are seeking healing, believe that you have just received it from Jesus. Why? Because that is what God promises in the Bible. Don't believe the symptoms in your body; they may still exist, but they don't have a right to exist! Deny them the right to exist and cast them out in Jesus's name.

Continue taking your medicine if you have it. Continue to follow your doctor's advice until your healing is confirmed by your doctor. This is the best witness of all. Your doctor exclaims, "I cannot understand how you were healed so quickly. It must be a miracle". Then you can tell your doctor about Jesus and have a great opportunity to be a witness for Jesus. Pray continually until all the symptoms are gone. Remember, Jesus had to pray twice for a blind man to receive his healing, so don't feel bad or lose faith simply because you must pray a number of times before your healing is seen and felt.

Here is a prayer for healing that you can use. Insert the sickness or condition in the blank space.

> Dear God, I come to you as a born-again believer in Jesus Christ, I claim Him as my personal Lord and Savior. I believe that you raised Him from the dead

and that now He sits at your right hand in heaven. In His name I believe that I receive healing for [say the sickness or condition] that is attacking my body. I declare it a trespasser and cast out the spirit which is causing this condition, right now! My body is the temple of the Holy Spirit, and I will not have it defiled with sickness. By Jesus's stripes, I was healed. This means that it was done two thousand years ago. I am healed now because Jesus is the same yesterday, today, and forever.

Thank You, God, for the promises in Your Word. I will walk in faith. I forgive those I may be mad at or have something against. Thank You for my healing, and I praise You for my healing, and I will continuously thank You until all symptoms disappear. Then I will thank You that it is done. I will tell someone what Jesus did for me. In His name I pray, amen.

Next, get into a church where you hear preaching about God's healing power. Find a place where they openly lay hands on people and expect God's Word to be done. If you surround yourself with people who believe and act on God's Word, you will be much better able to receive and keep your healing. If religious practice, unbelief, or tradition in a church teaches that the gifts of the Spirit like healing are not for today, then healing might not happen. Jesus Himself was prevented from doing great miracles in his home town because they refused to believe in Him (Matthew 13:53–58). If a church doesn't believe, they probably won't receive all God has for them.

Read what God has to say about folks like this in Galatians 1:8: It is impossible to improve upon Paul's message from God on the subject of preaching of a compromised or incomplete Gospel.

END OF TRACT

LESSON 6

DELIVERANCE

In John 10:10, Jesus tells us that the devil comes to __ _____

_____ but Jesus came and provided the Holy

Spirit so that we _____
(my paraphrase). Because the devil is not a human being but a Spirit being, the only way he can harm anyone is by spiritual means. The ministry of deliverance seeks to drive these spirits away from the one they are influencing or controlling.

In John 6:38 Jesus said, "I came down from Heaven not to mine own will, but in Him that sent me." The deliverance miracles that Jesus did were God's will in action. Jesus said that we would do greater works in His name than even he did. Read John 14:12. It is unfortunate that arguments over whether a Christian can be possessed of a devil or oppressed by a spirit have taken precedence over the ministry that gets rid of them! There are those who would rather argue semantics than deliver ministry to those in need.

In this segment of the exhorter training, we will give you a very basic overview of what deliverance is all about, and we'll get you to a place where you can pray with a person for deliverance and in faith expect that it will happen. Please read the lesson and study the Bible verses. In the next meeting, people will be expected to share their experiences or inexperience in deliverance. Remember that deliverance is a part of praying for many needs. We have all heard of spirits of illness and fear getting in the way of a Christian's walk with Jesus. We pray for these things all the time. Now we are going to do a brief study of it so you can become better equipped to do what God puts in your path to do.

In biblical times, there were many gods worshiped by various populations. The same is true today in parts of the world where voodoo and other forms of occult are practiced. There were even household gods just for a single family. After the Christian reformation, many former worshipers of multiple gods substituted angels or saints as persons to pray to. These populations believed in a spirit world as a normal thing. In the Caribbean and Africa today, lots of people believe in the spirit world as a normal, everyday thing.

Modern Westerners are not taught of the spirit world. Some may have academic knowledge that God is a Spirit, and that there is a Holy Spirit. They have probably heard of voodoo, and nearly everyone has heard of Satan. But grasping the fact that there is a spirit world running along with our temporal world is a hard concept to understand for modern, "sophisticated," educated people.

The negative influence of spirits under the command of Satan is either denied or ignored by many Christians. Their denomination has not taught them about spiritual warfare, using excuses like "This went out when the disciples died off." They excuse the influence of demon spirits as psychological defects or mental illness. Some churches skip over any text that could be controversial. Others may even teach that deliverance is some kind of occult counterfeit of Christianity. Wow, how wrong can they be? It is a fact that Ephesians 6:12 is inoperative in some churches: "that we war not against flesh and blood (people), but against the rulers, against the authorities, against the powers of this dark world, and against the spiritual forces of evil in the heavenly realms." In verse 18, after some instructions about the full armor of God, the Word says, "And pray in the spirit on all occasions with all kinds of prayers and requests."

In this church, we believe in the Word of God we read in the Bible. As you will see, driving out spirits is a biblical mandate for all of us. In Acts 5:15, the early Christians prayed and healed the sick and drove out evil spirits. Nothing in the Bible suggests that we are to do any differently today. Clearly, not taking up physical arms against a foe is a spiritual warfare situation. As I said in our last lesson, believe what the Bible says. You must reject what your experience, your feelings, or your religion teaches you if it does not line up with God's Word. If any statement, teaching, or belief is counter to God's Word, then it is wrong and should be rejected as a lie. Deliverance, like healing and salvation, is for today.

As Christian workers, we will be asked many questions about the Bible. We will not know all the answers, so we must exhort the questioner to read the Bible and discover the answers. This is not a cop-out. We must be diligent and lovingly guide them to the portions of the Bible (in context) that provide the answer. Knowing how to use a concordance and Bible dictionary are helpful skills.

One big question will be, "Can a Christian be demon possessed?" The short answer is no. Possession is having total ownership and total control. As Christians, we belong to God, so Satan cannot gain total control. Can non-Christians yield total control? Most likely. In Mark 1:23–25, Jesus encounters a man "possessed" by a spirit, and He casts it out. The examples we read about in the Bible of people possessed by demons are not born-again Christians.

However, my advice is to avoid a discussion of semantics. Arguing whether a condition or situation is possession, oppression, undue influence, or any other word for "messing with our lives, health, and happiness" is useless chatter. We can cast out the spirit no matter if the person in trouble is a Christian or an unsaved person. It makes no difference if the spirit oppressed them or possessed them. It doesn't matter whether it's inside them, next to them, on them, or whispering in their ear. None of these semantic issues makes any difference; once we cast it out, the problem is solved.

Modern scholars are substituting the word *demonized*, a transliteration of the Greek word *daimonizomai* which had been translated as "demon possession" in early translations of the Bible. Using this substitute word avoids the inevitable arguments about possession and oppression. What is possible is for Christians to yield some control over themselves to demon spirits in much the same way they could yield to a sin like alcoholism or drug addiction.

Proof of this is when Paul warns in Ephesians 4:27 not to give the devil a foothold. Paul would not preach about it if it were not possible for the demon to "gain a foothold" to cause us problems. This admonition is to not to let demonic spirits into our space. Foothold in the Greek means inhabitable space, like a room in one's house. So we must guard our space, minds, emotions, and fleshly tendencies against the spirits noted in Ephesians 6. Christians can give him a foothold. How many Christians have committed adultery, gone to jail for a crime, or done something else that gave glory to the devil and not to God?

In Job 1:6–8, Satan is described as a fallen angel (one of the sons of God) who roamed the earth and had power over things on it. Revelation 12:9 informs us that in earlier history (pre-Adam), the devil and his angels were cast out of heaven onto earth. Jesus describes it vividly in Luke 10:18, and He actually saw Satan cast down to the earth like lightning. Satan and his spirits are still here! Deliverance is the method we use to get him away from Christians and others so that overcoming life can be enjoyed by all.

Because of Adam's fall, we are born sinners and have to receive salvation at some point in our lives to be saved from eternal damnation. We live in a sinful world. Why is it a sinful world? Because the devil is the god of it. We can overcome the devil by the power of the Holy Spirit, promised to us by Jesus Christ.

Our goal is to disciple each other and live in Christian community with each other. When needed, we are to cast out spirits or demons that are causing trouble. Therefore, in answer to this possession or oppression question, or one like it, we explain it as follows: Satan is called the god of this world in 2 Corinthians 4:4. We are temporary residents here on earth until we get to go to heaven and be with Jesus. While we are here, Satan's demonic spirits will seek to do his work of stealing, killing, and destroying Christians (and others).

Without getting into the semantics of possession and oppression, you can guide the discussion to getting down to solving a problem. In Matthew 16:18, Christ says that "on this rock [the Holy Spirit] I will build my Church and the gates of hell will not prevail against it." We have the power because Jesus gave it to us. James 4:7 says we are to submit ourselves to God; resist the devil and he will (not may) flee from you.

You cannot see Satan; he is a spirit, as are his cohorts the fallen angels. They must work in the spirit realm to cause things to happen in the temporal realm. Hence they work on our minds and our fleshly instincts, tempting us, beguiling us, and propagandizing us with sinful music and entertainment. Revelation 16:14 tells us that in the last days, spirits of demons will inhabit world leaders. They will try to inhabit you now, but they cannot. In Colossians 2:15 Jesus spoiled principalities and powers; He made a show of them openly, triumphing over them. He defeated them, and He gave you power in the Holy Spirit, so you win.

However, as long as we live on earth, we will have to wage continual battle with Satan and his evil spirits. Let's move on and get into a place where we are comfortable with our rights and privileges in Jesus Christ, a place where we can confidently pray with someone and cast out evil spirits that are interfering with our lives.

One of the principal ways Satan can gain a foothold is the mind, Satan can move in your imagination. He can use suggestion through literature, listening to gossip, sinful entertainment, and more. He can exert control a little bit at a time. He doesn't need to possess anyone; he only needs to exert enough control to get you out of God's will and into the self. When he gets Christ out of your thoughts, he wins. It makes no difference if you get into sinful activities or just go overboard on physical fitness. Once your mind is off Christ, the devil wins.

In Philippians 4:6, Paul says we need not be anxious about things, but by prayer and petition and in thanks bring our requests to God. When we do, the peace which passes all understanding will guard our hearts and minds in Christ Jesus. In verse 8, Paul admonishes us to think on things that are true, honest, just, pure, lovely, and things of good report. Don't be bugged about negative things; think on God's Word and His blessings, and guard your mind. If you do so, the devil cannot get a foothold.

These are points we have to get across to the person we are praying with. This deliverance session is not a one-time event. It is a process that begins with the binding and casting out of the spirit. Then we go to Romans 12:2: "be not conformed to this world but be transformed by the renewing of your MIND." Look also at 2 Corinthians 10:4.The weapons of our warfare are not carnal or worldly, but mighty through divine power to bring down strongholds.

Exhort people that good things must go in their minds through their eyes and ears, and good things must come out of their mouths. It's the divine GIGO concept: garbage in, garbage out, or, in God's terms, "good in, good out." Jesus explains this in Luke 6:45.

Going back to 1 Corinthians, to the last part of verse 5: "we take captive every thought to make it obedient to Christ." People must see that the process is a renewing of their minds and a change in their way of life to conform with a Godly example instead of a worldly example. Reading the Bible and seeking God's answers will give them peace.

We can bind and cast out spirits, but the job is not done. We must assure ourselves that the person is sincere in wanting the spirits out, and that they will commit to a different sort of lifestyle, one that denies spirits a place (room in the house) to exist. Then we need to see to it that there is follow-up to disciple the person in the Word. Get them in a church or Bible study; they need to fill themselves with God things. This will fill the void left by the evil spirits and the inappropriate behavior that previously inhabited their minds or bodies.

Jesus is clear what will happen if the person is not committed to getting rid of the spirit. If they are insincere when they pray, "When an unclean spirit goes out of a man, he goes through dry places, seeking rest, and finds none. Then he says, 'I will return to my house from which I came.' And when he comes, he finds *it* empty, swept, and put in order. Then he goes and takes with him seven other spirits more wicked than himself, and they enter and dwell there; and the last *state* of that man is worse than the first. So shall it also be with this wicked generation" (Matthew 12:43–45). Wow! If we jump to pray a spirit out of a person, if the timing is not right, or if instruction in righteousness is not given and received, then seven worse spirits can enter the person! This is not my opinion—this is the Word of Christ!

The ministry of deliverance is a duty of all of us. Mark 16:17 admonishes us to go out, witness Jesus Christ, and cast out demons. But having the power and duty is like having the keys to a car and not knowing how to drive. We have studied the topic of deliverance; now let's get down to some practicalities.

Are you truly mature in your own walk with Christ? Are you practicing a godly life as best you can? Do you regularly read and study your Bible? Do godly things mean more to you than worldly things? Look at your calendar and checkbook; are a significant part of your time and resources spent on God? Do you feel secure in your walk with Jesus? Can you witness without timidity and continue praying without making excuses when prayers are not immediately answered?

Are you free from habits that don't glorify God? These habits include smoking, drinking, drugs, pornography, lust, bad spending habits, failure to discipline children, marital discord, and financial irresponsibility. We must clean ourselves up before cleaning others. Our code of conduct is a benchmark we all must conform to in this church.

Next, before praying for someone, be "prayed up" yourself. I heard one preacher say that he prayed in the Spirit for a number of hours before ever ministering. Jesus explains this to the disciples in Mark 9:29. He clearly states that being "prayed up" is required to harness the power to cast out some devils. If Jesus had to stay prayed up, we sure do! You need to know that you are ready to do spiritual warfare.

We all live everyday in a temporal world; we drive, we eat, and we see things and people. We do not regularly confront spirits. So when we are planning to get in a fight with one or more spirits, we had better be prayed up and operating in a spiritual state, not a natural state. Instead of listening to oldies on the radio, have a praise tape or a study tape on in the car. Keep the good things going in your eyes and ears so that you will be ready to act when needed. As 2 Timothy 4:2 states, be ready in and out of season.

Jesus quickly discerned evil spirits and cast them out. We need to be operating in the spirit so we can identify them and cast them out if it's appropriate at that time. We have to discern the motives of the person, the attitude, the commitment to a changed life, and the spirit. It's a big job for a truck driver or an office worker, but perhaps it's easier for a carpenter!

If you have time beforehand, you should do the same thing that the intercessory prayer people do every Sunday at the church. Pray over the place you are meeting, casting out any spirits that would interfere with God's work. Pray for an anointing on yourself and anyone assisting you. If someone is available to intercede for you during the course of the session, that is a plus. We make this same duty normal for ushers during a prayer service; they always intercede for the people at the altar.

Some churches have a team of three people praying for the service in another room during the service. You can arrange for this if you know you're going to be praying for someone; call and have two or three people praying for you at home, to gird you up during the deliverance session.

The last item in preparation is a firm belief in your mind that you have the right and the power (2 Corinthians 10:4) to do what is needed in the situation that is causing the person problems. If you are timid or unsure of yourself, get some help. Matthew 18:19 says where two agree about anything you ask for, it will be done for you by the Father in heaven. Jesus advises that two are better than one.

Let's review.

- You are in good spiritual condition.
- You are prayed up; ask for discerning of spirits.
- You believe that you will receive from Christ, through the Holy Spirit, the direction to pray for the person in need.
- You have someone interceding for you and the situation.

Your best tools in a session of deliverance are your ears. Listen to people. Get them talking about the situation. There may be biblical answers to a problem that has nothing to do with an evil spirit. Exhort them with appropriate Bible scriptures that address the situation—scriptures on marriage, on money, or on raising kids.

People may be involved in dumb conduct that is obvious without any spiritual discernment at all (drinking, dope, etc.). They may be making bad judgments. Yes, they may be assisted by Satanic spirits, but not necessarily. As God's creations, we have free will. Some people do dumb things by their dumb will, not by spiritual influence. Satan wins in these cases, and he doesn't even have to put forth any effort!

If you discern that it is a spiritual problem, share your reasons with the people involved. Get them talking again, and wait for the Holy Spirit to reveal to you the way to pray. They may reveal something obvious; perhaps they are involved in some occult activity, or they have an addiction. Before praying the offending spirit out, make sure people are truly repentant of their sins, are committed to a lifestyle change, and are agreeable to be prayed for. Inform them if they do it frivolously and backslide, then the problem will be seven times worse.

This is not "fast food Christianity," a quick prayer and get on with life. This calls for a serious commitment on the part of the people desiring prayer. If you discern that they are ready, then pray with them. If not exhort, them to read the Bible and meet again another day.

First, solidify salvation. Take them through the sinner's prayer (whichever one you use) so you know that they are saved. Make sure they are not harboring unforgiveness, even for themselves. Matthew 6:14 says if we don't forgive others, God won't forgive us. Also, Mark 11:25 states we cannot harbor unforgiveness and expect forgiveness from God. People hating themselves for transgressions of the past is common and must be dealt with before deliverance.

Next, anoint them with oil (if you have it) and cast out the offending, trespassing, evil spirit forever! Speak to the spirit in authority and cast it out the way you would throw out a trespasser or burglar from your home. Tell it to get out!

Then attempt to lead them in baptism in the Holy Spirit. If they can receive this gift in faith and begin to speak in tongues, they have a large part of their battle won already. Evil spirits cannot be in the same place as the Holy Spirit. If they get baptized in the Holy Spirit, it will enable them to pray in the Spirit and edify themselves and build their faith to continue to battle the devil from coming back after deliverance.

To sum up, we have learned that:

- There is a spirit world.
- Jesus gave us the gifts of the Holy Spirit, including the discerning of spirits, for a reason: to use them.
- Spirits can cause people problems, and the unsaved can even be possessed totally by them. The saved cannot be possessed, but they can be negatively influenced by them.
- We need to live good Christian lives and be prayed up to be prepared for the task of praying out spirits.
- We need to disciple, to assist those we pray with so they will not backslide and get seven times more problems.

Homework: Read ahead in lesson 8 and look up the scriptures. Bring in a question that will interest others.

MOTIVATIONAL GIFTS I AND II

The gifts that will be the subject of the next two meetings are those in Romans 12:3–7. They are commonly called the motivational or foundational gifts; they could also be called personality gifts. The reason is because the way we move in the gifts we are given are how others perceive us, and to an extent, how we perceive ourselves.

Secular psychologists and salesmanship teachers have other names for these gifts. In short, they are the attitudes and motivations that we naturally operate in as we go through life. The manner in which we approach and solve problems, interact with people, and choose a occupation or profession will be greatly influenced by the gift that is primary in each of our lives.

Most agree that no person is simply one gift. We are all a combination of gifts. However, one will stand out; we call that the primary gift. Our objective in this class is to acquaint you with the gifts, discuss them briefly, and contrast them with other types of gifts mentioned in the Bible. As Christians, it is important to know what our gifts are. We should be able to recognize another's gift so we can be more effective in witnessing to them and discipling them.

A study of the motivational gifts must begin with a short overview of other gifts so confusion will not occur with similar names. Your responsibility is to read the various scriptures and this lesson. Be ready to discuss these motivational gifts in the context of getting people saved, baptized in the Holy Spirit, healing, and deliverance.

Review lessons 3–6 so that you will be ready to discuss how knowing the motivational gifts will help you to be a better witness. Your instructor will go over the fill-in spots in your manual during the introduction. Later during the classes, we may compare a gift from Romans 12 with a ministerial gift in Ephesians 4, and also with the Holy Spirit gifts in 1 Corinthians 12. We will see similar terms used, but the meanings are different.

First look up Ephesians 4:10–11 and review the ministerial gifts God has given to lead the Church. Remember these are referred to in the modern world as ministers, missionaries, and pastors.

Apostles. Meaning "_____". Like a missionary or a church planter. People who are sent from place to place with a charge from the Church to accomplish a task, usually to start a new work, raise up leadership, and then move on. The word in Greek is *apostolos*.

Prophets. Divine philosophers, they point to the _____ or _____ and make a point or _____ for God. Like Moses. The word in Greek is *prophetes*.

Evangelist. Stirs things up. Attracts by _____. Brings _____ as compared with the prophet, who may not bring glad tidings. The word in the Greek is *euangelistes*.

Pastors. Translated _____ once, _____ sixteen times in the New Testament. In Hebrew, *Ra'ha* is translated to pastor eight times and shepherd sixty-three times in the Old Testament. The word in Greek is *poimen*.

Teacher. Teachers of _____in the churches. The word in Greek is *didaskalos*.

These are commonly referred to as the "fivefold ministry gifts." They are terms associated with people who hold an office in vocational ministry. Mostly these people are ordained or licensed individuals who have answered the call to leadership in the Church.

The next grouping of gifts are the Holy Spirit gifts, which are given to all Christians who ask for them. These are sometimes called the charismatic gifts. These are not offices like the fivefold ministry gifts. These are power gifts promised to us by Jesus himself. See 1 Corinthians 12, and start at verse 8.

The three "revelation gifts"	The "power" gifts	The "spoken" gifts,
Word of knowledge v-8	Faith v-9	Diverse kinds of tongues (public or private) v-10
Word of wisdom v-8	Miracles v-10	Interpretation of tongues (usually public) v-10
Discerning of spirits v-10	Healings v-9	Prophesy v-10

These are the gifts referred to when someone exclaims that the congregation moved in the Spirit, or moved in body life. These are the gifts the people who were in Corinth were misusing when Paul had to instruct them in 1 Corinthians chapters 12–14.

The next two classes are on how to use the motivational, foundational, or personality gifts—whatever you choose to call them—in order to be a better witness. Read Romans Chapter 12 and start at verse 3. Go over any footnotes in your Bible.

Prophesy. Draw an eye. This person likes to identify motives. He is very direct, and things are usually seen as black-and-white. In Greek it is *propheteia*. Make some notes on how you might witness salvation (or healing, or anything else) to this type person.

Gift of Ministry. From the Greek *diakona*. Do practical needs—janitor, cook, carpenter, audio visual. A helper type. Draw a hand. For this one, use your imagination on how to witness to her. What might be hard or easy?

Gift of Teacher. Very into the Word. Everything is "Word this" and "Word that." Draw an ear. These people hear the Word and have to tell everyone about it. From the Greek *didasco*, meaning "to give instruction.' Make a note or two on what challenges or opportunities this gift presents to you.

Gift of Exhortation. This person loves to help people through situations, to give spiritual advice, and to encourage spiritual growth, and he loves people. He is always there, like a tree. So draw a tree and make notes.

Gift of Giving. Loves to give, makes money, and shares it generously with others. Likes to involve others in giving. Draw a dollar sign and make notes.

Gift of Organizer. Also known as ruler in the King James Version. Sets goals and motivates others to attain those goals. Draw a head. Make notes.

Gift of Mercy. Identifies emotional needs and wounds and tries to patch them up. Draw a heart for this one. This should be the easiest to think of ways to witness.

For two weeks, we will be discussing all of these gifts and how they need to be taken into consideration not only when you are choosing and evaluating helps workers, but when witnessing. These two classes will be a chance for everyone to get up to speed on salvation, baptism in the Holy Spirit, healing, and deliverance.

Someone who may have an entirely different motivational gift than you do will approach a task in a vastly different way. Hopefully these two classes will give you perspective on how to better get along. Another thing that can be an irritant to you and to others is that a goal that is of high importance to you may be insignificant to another. Knowing motivational gifts can avoid confrontations and disagreements.

I think you will all agree that understanding both people's perspectives will go a long way in keeping the peace and gaining the cooperation of others. Many Christians have mistaken the actions of someone working merrily in his gift as a direct insult to them when it is contrary to their motivational gift. We will illustrate some examples of potential conflicts as the discussion moves on.

Let us use an imaginary volunteer work program at a church for our examples and discussion.

THE HIGHLY RELIGIOUS CHURCH OF MISCOMMUNICATION

We are going to discuss some "real" Helps workers and see where things are going right and wrong. For the first couple of weeks, the church had its volunteer worker program. Everything went okay, and then interest waned. At the end of the first month, there aren't enough workers left to get the jobs done on time.

We will pretend to listen in on a group of the volunteers planning how to get some others in the church to join in their efforts and get things back on track. Hopefully this imaginary conversation will illustrate to us how saints with differing motivational gifts approach the same challenge.

Pete the Prophet jumps up, waves his arms, and declares, "We need to contact each and every one of the people who signed up to work, confronting them with their lack of responsibility to God's work. By golly, they signed up, and now they will have to live up to it or wander in the wilderness for forty years!"

Manny the Minister says, "Wait. If we all just work a little harder, we can get it done." Then he proceeds to work all night on the project.

Tom the Teacher says, "Well, that might work. The Word says we can do all things through Christ that strengthens us. However, the Word also says those that don't work don't get to eat. So why should we do their share of the work?"

Eric the Exhorter decides to drop by each person's home and tell them how much they are missed, how rewarding the work is, and how important to the kingdom it is. He intends to uplift and encourage them back into the group.

Greg the Giver suggests, "We should take up a special offering to have the job done professionally." He personally seeds one hundred dollars as an encouragement for others to join in the effort.

Oliver the rganizer" laments that if he had been in charge from the first, he would have had a second and possibly a third backup plan. There would have been a schedule of when and where to report, and what to do. Further, a phone notification would have reminded and encouraged people to show up. Lastly, if there were a problem, he would have had a backup group of workers or a professional in place to get the job done.

Martin the Merciful says, "Let's calm down. We need to try to figure out why the folks did not show up. Perhaps there was sickness in the family we need to pray about. These are good people;, I'm sure they just forgot. Let's not be judgmental."

These examples are perhaps not too realistic, but they are overboard examples of how the seven motivational types might react to the same problem. A variation on this has probably happened in every church. We see varying reactions from people who live in a certain gift. In the class discussion, you can build on this silly example and use your imagination to transfer the example to when you might be witnessing to someone.

It's easy to see how people perceived this lack of participation in vastly differing ways. Yet none of them know for sure why the people did not show up. They all have a solution. Any of the solutions could be correct for one individual, but it would be grossly inappropriate for someone else. In witnessing, you can see how being unaware of a motivational gift might put you at a disadvantage, and another person who recognized the gift could be more effective.

Can we see how easy it would be for Pete the Prophet to feel that Martin the Merciful is too soft, or that all Tom the Teacher does is spout the Word and never get anything practical done?

Eric the Exhorter might consider that Pete the Prophet is just a frustrated first sergeant, always pushing his weight around.

They all might consider Oliver the Organizer lazy; he just writes stuff down and never wants to get his hands dirty. Gilbert the Giver might be in for some flak because he isn't in the thick of the work. What they don't see is that he needs to work more overtime to generate the extra money he is giving.

Tom the Teacher might quietly look at the whole bunch of them and lament, "If they were all in the Word enough, God would supply the answer." Then we have Manual the Minister working diligently and grumbling to himself, "If these people would quit discussing things and get to work, maybe we could get this job done before midnight!"

You can see how we could carry out these examples to include all seven, and to have some arguments. Perhaps in your church life, you have experienced some of these frustrations and the resulting hurt feelings. Hopefully once you have finished these two lessons, you will have a greater appreciation for the differing gifts, and you'll develop an ability to effectively work with the differing types of motivation gifts.

The basic objective of this entire course is to win souls to Christ. The unsaved have these same motivations, so knowing them and appreciating them will make you a more effective witness of the Gospel.

Pastors and ministry leaders must know the motivations of those working for them so that duties and responsibilities can be assigned correctly and effectively.

FAITHFULNESS AND COMMITMENT

As you do the homework, you will see how many times God's Word gives us practical examples of people who were faithful to their duties. It will be an inspiration to all of us in our church work and on our jobs.

Scripture references follow on the next page. Your assignment is to look them up and make appropriate notes for each one. Next week, we will discuss them in class, and everyone will have an opportunity to share answers to one or more of the questions.

FAITHFULNESS SCRIPTURES

Numbers 12:7. Who was faithful in all things? _____

1 Samuel 2:35. Who is the faithful priest? _____

1 Samuel 22:14. Who was honorable in the king's house? _____

Nehemiah 13:13. What do we call these people today? _____

Proverbs 14:5 This scripture tells us to tell the _____ or _____
_____.

Proverbs 28:20. The faithful get _____; the moneygrubbers get _____.

Isaiah 8:2. What did the faithful witnesses do? _____, and _____ in _____.

Isaiah 25:1. What are God's Counsels of Old? _____ and _____

Jeremiah 23:28. Concerning speaking the Word, give your thoughts on this scripture. The Hebrew word is _____ or trustworthiness

Matthew 24:45. Who was ruler over an entire household? _____

Matthew 25:21 & 23. Why did the servants get rewarded? _____

Ephesians 6:21. Tychicus was a _____.

1 Timothy 1:12. Jesus counted Paul _____ and put him _____ the _____.

2 Timothy 2:2. What must faithful men do here? _____ _____ _____ _____ _____.

3 John 5. Doing _____ whatever we can for the Church and for others.

Answer the question. What does it matter if we are faithful or not? God forgives us. Write in some comments for discussion next week.

CHURCH GOVERNMENT

The primary issues facing us as Christians in the twenty-first century are:

- How do we operate our churches in a way that is pleasing to God?
- How do we do it with a guide book, the last chapter of which was written two thousand years ago?
- How do we do it in a way that complies with the secular governments rules for "exempt status"?

Before we can get into the details of the structure, we must get one primary precept clear in our minds. Without understanding this, no serious study of church government can be held.

God is sovereign, and His Word is absolute truth. From Genesis, where He created everything by His Word, there was no interference by a deacon board or by a vote. In the New Testament, He manifested Himself in the flesh as Jesus. Then, even over the protestations of His elders (Matt. 16:22–23), there was never a vote or a discussion. For Jesus's ministry on earth and afterword during the ministry of the apostles, we find no evidence to suggest that elders, deacons, or bishops ever had any control over the apostles or their appointed preachers (what we call the fivefold ministry today). That is what the Bible teaches us, not man's opinion or invention. We'll hear about them shortly.

The primary concept or precept that has to be understood is that _____

_____

The second concept is longer than the first:_____

_____

_____

_____

This sounds simple and obvious, but here is where many arguments and disagreements occur. For example, pulpit placement, decoration of churches, clergy apparel—all these things have had Christians at each other's throats, with people thinking the others are less Christian because of their stances on these issues. We are here to do God's work, not argue about things like this.

The key is understanding the differences and then appreciating that there is a place in God's scheme of things for:

- The things He has ordained (precept 1)
- The things He leaves for us to sort out (precept 2)

Once we have this clear in our minds, we can go on and study church government with a new freedom of understanding.

It is not small stuff. Denominations have risen and fallen by "majoring on the minors." Arguments over issues God is silent upon have created rules and laws in churches that God never intended. Even today, you can get thrown out of Jesus-believing churches for violating a denominational rule or tradition. We do not judge churches for this; we merely point out that there are two sets of rules, God's and man's. We do not ignore man's rules; rather, we must consider them in the context of God's Word. If they do not violate His Word, then they may be okay. If they compliment and uplift God's Word, they are okay.

God's Word admonishes us to obey those who have rule over us, and Romans chapter 13 is a good example of this. Man will create rules, which are necessary for order. I suggest that if God's rules get first place in your church, and if you diligently read God's Word, then as time passes, the flaky ecclesiastical law will fall to the wayside from lack of attention. Do not criticize other denominations or churches, or joke about their traditions. Concentrate on uplifting Jesus in your life and let them attend to their lives.

By joining a denomination, you pledge to follow the rules of that church. That is all right, but realize that they are man's rules as you follow them. If you make a mistake, repent, ask for forgiveness, and carry on with life. Hebrews 13:17 also exhorts us to obey those that have rule over us. That includes our parents, our pastors and leaders, our bosses at work, and our denominations.

Ephesians 4:11–13 tells us that our preachers are a gift from God; surely we can submit to them. Also, 1 Corinthians 1:10 admonishes us to speak in one accord; this can be all of us obeying the rules! Let's remember these basics as we study Church government.

Four Basic Types of Church Government

_____ From the Greek word *Episcopos*, which means bishop or overseer. This is where the pastor has a bishop or overseer supervising him. Here, the local pastor has less control over what happens in the church, as is evidenced in the Catholic and Episcopal denominations, where there is a liturgy from which pastors are not supposed to deviate during services. Churches are usually not owned locally but by the denomination; property cannot be purchased or sold except with the approval of the bishop or overseer. In some cases, the local congregation might have some small say in the selection of their pastor, but the final decision is always with the bishop or overseer.

_____ From the Greek *Presbuteros*, or elder. The words *presbyter*, *bishop* (In Greek, *Episkopos*) and *deacon* (in Greek, *Diakoneo*) were common official titles used for leaders in secular society at that time. Nearly everyone in society had one of these types of folks supervising them, and they knew that they had to follow the orders given. It was natural for the early Church to adopt them as easily recognized words for leaders in the Church. These position titles have stayed permanently in the Church and have fallen out of use in secular society. In this form of government, the presbyters (or business leaders) have the responsibility to operate the church and hire the pastor. Presbyterians use this method, and others use variations of it.

_____ This third type has great favor in the United States. It is how we run our secular government and is very popular with a people who value their freedom. The congregation votes on major issues, including hiring or firing a pastor, purchasing or selling property, and who can be a member. Speculation is that this form of Church government prospered because so many of our citizens are immigrants from nations where the government controlled the Church. In many cases, there was religious discrimination or suppression in their former countries. When they got here, having a say in the Church seemed a good thing to them. Today, great denominations such as the Assemblies of God, most of the Baptist denominations, and other denominations use forms of this government.

This form of government is impossible to justify with the Word of God. There are no examples in the Old or New Testament of congregations starting churches or running them. All the examples are of the Levitical priesthood running the synagogues in the Old Testament, and the apostles and their appointed leaders running the New Testament churches. The apostles appointed elders and leaders, not the other way around. This does not make these churches bad, and neither does it detract from the good they have done and continue to do. Sometimes church politics gets in the way of what God is trying to do, taking people's minds off God.

The challenge for people in these churches is being diligent in seeking God when they vote. Consider the candidates in the context of the Bible, not a popularity contest. Use Acts 6:3. Pretend you are an apostle and chose people who are honest, full of the Holy Spirit, and wise to appoint over the church.

The last form of government is the _____. In this form of government, the pastor, evangelist, or person in charge of the ministry is in fact the head over everything. Any elders, deacons, or other advisors are chosen by that person and serve at his pleasure.

Examples of this form of government is found in the ministry of Moses, who chose his own judges (with no vote), and Elijah, who chose his own successor (without a vote or consultation with a board). All the Old Testament prophets and the New Testament apostles followed God's direction for their lives and ministries. All were led by the Holy Spirit, not a deacon board. If we examine the organization of Jesus's ministry, we find the same pattern. Jesus ran the show and appointed those of His own choosing to positions of authority.

In those days, one frequently saw examples of those who did not like what the prophet said. The prophet still stayed the prophet; no one fired him or her. Today, many independent churches function this way.

Many pastors do not have a business background and rely heavily on church elders for advice. In the congregational and Presbyterian forms of government, the pastor may be obliged or required to take the advice of the elders. In the Episcopal and independent forms, they may take it or not as they wish.

God has given us free will. He desires us to praise Him and honor Him. One of the ways we honor God is by honoring His gift to us: our pastors (and others in ministry). Although we may feel more comfortable having control over our pastors with a vote, this has nothing to do with God's way of doing business. Some churches even have pulpit committees to "suggest" to the pastor what should be preached!

In 1 Timothy 6:20–21, Paul gives Timothy an admonition. Grant me the privilege of embellishing it: "O Timothy, keep God's Word and keep his congregation, which is committed to your trust. Avoid profane babbling and contradictions of what is called knowledge (like arguments with the church boards and elders), especially when those profess scientific knowledge superior to the pastor and which strays from the faith." Ask for examples from the class.

Let's do a brief recap.

What are the two precepts we must keep in mind?

- Christianity is not a democracy.
- All things concerning operation of a church are not answered in the Bible.

The four forms of government

- Episcopal
- Presbyterian
- Congregational
- Independent

The name of our church is: _____ _____

Next, what are some of the things the typical denominational church does to get organized? Take these steps so that people who come from another church can expect the same statements of faith and standards of worship.

- Organize a structure that can govern a large, multinational organization.
- License and ordain clergy so that there is a standard known to all.
- Establish churches or merge established churches who wish to join them.
- Establish, own, and operate educational institutions of collegiate and less than collegiate grade.
- Establish, maintain, and conduct missionary endeavors for the furtherance of the Gospel in the United States and the world.
- Do other things needed in furtherance of the Gospel.

The following are the offices that govern our church or our denomination if affiliated with one.

DISCIPLINE, ORGANIZATION, AND STAFF RELATIONSHIPS IN THE LOCAL BODY

This is a continuation of the last lesson. We now move to the local level. Pastors appoint support people to one-year terms to assist in the ministry to the local congregation. Some of those offices are:

_____ _____ One who is related in function to the senior pastor. Second overseer of the entire congregation. This position takes the broad view of the congregation and church as a body.

_____ _____ These ministers are more specialized. They may oversee a function or a group of functions: music, children's pastor, youth pastor, administrators, minister of visitation, and others. All licensed and ordained clergy serving a pastor must resign when that pastor leaves, thus leaving the new pastor with the freedom to appoint leaders they have selected in accordance with Acts 6:3.

Pastors also hire clerical and administrative and maintenance people to run secular operations at a church. These jobs are generally filled by church members, but they are not usually licensed or ordained, and they typically do not have to resign their jobs when there is a change of pastor.

In each church, the pastor has the ultimate responsibility for all functions. Thus everyone performing jobs in those various functions must subordinate themselves to the pastor (if your church by-laws provide for this). He and only he has to take the heat if people mess up, so he has to have the authority and power to supervise others in whatever jobs they have. This is usually done by creating an organizational chart and delegating responsibility and authority to assistants and leaders in various functions.

For example, when the leader of the audio visual department gives direction to one of the workers in that department, it is the same as if the pastor gave the direction. Following that instruction is not subject to debate or argument—you just do it. We do things we don't really enjoy in our secular jobs. Some parts of every job are tedious, but someone has to do it. Likewise in the church, a leader may ask you to do something you aren't thrilled about. Show your love of God by doing the task without comment, particularly if it is during a service. There is no time for debate when the service is going on.

Maintain and respect the organizational structure. Let supervisors supervise, and refrain from jumping in and correcting a worker who is assigned to another leader. Tell the leader privately, and let him or her handle the training or discipline. Unless there is danger to someone, do not interfere with another person's job. As leaders, we must be instant in season to assist anywhere we are needed, including cleaning toilets if that is necessary. Jesus washed feet, so we can clean toilets. We must demonstrate to the congregation that we are servants, not bosses. We cannot be perceived as being too good to do something.

Matthew 18:15 gives specific instruction as to how disagreements are to be handled. In the Helps ministry, the witnesses should be other members of your ministry group who agree with you. Taking it to the Church is going up another level, to the immediate supervisor of your supervisor. You only go to the pastor if that person is your supervisor's supervisor. Differences of opinion between workers should not be discussed with spouses, children, or others who can spread gossip. Let's resolve disagreements in the Helps ministry—*in* the ministry—not bring disputes into the congregation.

- 1 Peter 8:3–13 is our Bible reference for the above. Let's be in one accord, speaking well of one another, not speaking evil of anyone. Peter is speaking to us here.
- Hebrews 13:17 admonishes us to obey those who have rule over us.

Elsewhere in the word, we are told to "esteem our leaders highly in love." Let's see how God wants us to feel love and esteem. Beseech in this context is stronger than asking like a child would to a parent, and it's not an order; rather, it is an asking from a equal to an equal. Here we have Paul beseeching us, talking to us as an equal (1 Thessalonians 5:12–13).

Here is one addressed to pastors and spiritual leaders (1 Peter 5:1–3). He uses the term *elder*, and in this context the Greek is *Sumpresbuteros* (fellow elder), not just plain *presbuteros*, which is an elder. He uses the familiar "fellow elder." Imagine: a fellow elder with a guy like Peter, the man from the inner circle of Jesus Himself! He's not just a plain, old elder. "Shepherd the flock of God which is among you, serving as overseers, not by compulsion but willingly, not for dishonest gain but eagerly; nor as being lords over those entrusted to you, but being examples to the flock; and when the Chief Shepherd appears, you will receive the crown of glory that does not fade away."

For an example of organization, look at what Jesus accomplished in three years. He ran his ministry and did not back off from any challenge. He was fearless. We must be so, even in the face of adversity.

- He appointed three assistant or associate pastors to help Him: Peter, James, and John. Our pastor is doing this.
- He had a leadership team of the twelve (including the senior staff). We have a church board and leaders in specific ministries
- He had a cadre of helpers—the seventy whom he trained and sent out. He later recharged them (Luke 10:1–20). This class is the first of many to equip you for future ministry.
- He set the example of multiplication, to spread the Word farther and faster. The apostles obviously got this message, because all except Judas Escariot went out, preached and taught, and started churches, which raised up preachers who did the same. We are the result of that process, which still goes on today. This class is an example of multiplication at work today.

Assignment: Read the next lesson and have some questions for next week.

HOW TO START A MINISTRY IN THE CHURCH

Proverbs 24:3–4 states, "A house is built by wisdom, and is set up by understanding. By discretion the chambers are filled with all precious and excellent wealth." this is translated from the Septuagint, the Greek translation of the Jewish Bible in use during Jesus's ministry.

Three key words. _____, _____ _____ and _____. Let's look at some places we've seen these words before. Turn to Acts 6:3. Do we remember how workers are chosen? Wasn't wisdom one of them? Let's remember 3 John 2, as we recall this was written to Gaius our big-time example of a successful and faithful Helps worker. Remember our souls are the minds, emotions, and intellect. When we develop a ministry outline, we want to use all the tools God gave us: the Word, wisdom, common sense, and knowledge of the technical (non-biblical) side of the ministry.

I have left a lot of room in the workbooks for you to jot down notes for a ministry you might want to start. The workbooks are yours; mark them up all you want.

Format for this chapter: *Everything in italics is instruction about the ministry outline.* What is written in regular type is the ministry outline.

The first thing is to write a paragraph or so, to let people know what is in the job description. Let them know the attitude needed for success.

Job Description for Ushering Ministry

Ushers are the most visible of workers during a service. They may take the offering, seat people, serve communion, and are generally more visible to the congregation. Thus you must represent God and the pastor and leadership of the church in an honorable way.

The best ushers are like waiters at a fancy restaurant: they seem to get everything done almost before you ask for it, and they do it in a way that you don't notice how hard they are working. In the church, Jesus gets the glory, and the pastor (or others in the pulpit) get the attention, not the ushers.

Here is a quick overview. List some jobs, seating, offering, or duties for that ministry. Say something about attitude, honor. Give an example everyone can relate to, and something about not being the center of attention.

The guidelines in this job description will assist you in performing outstanding service to God and the local body. They are not laws to be obeyed; they are a structure we use to insure everyone is in one accord. Acts 2:1 says if we are to expect baptisms in the Holy Spirit and other manifestations of the Spirit in our church, we must be in one accord. Also, instructions reduce the need for decision making, and things run smoother.

The third paragraph introduces the job description and gives a biblical basis for being organized "in one accord."

Many duties are required: turning on lights, adjusting heat, inspecting bathrooms, and more. Others require the leading of the Holy Spirit and presuppose that the usher is operating supernaturally on the job. An example would be someone throwing a noisy fit during the sermon. When do you remove them? What do you say to them? Where do you take them? You won't find the answers written here. The Holy Spirit must take charge then. Your pastor or another in the pulpit may have the unction of the Holy Spirit and give direction, but you will do the work and you will say the words. So be prayed up, operate in love, and maintain an attitude of a servant not an enforcer of the rules (Philippians 2:2–4).

The final paragraph suggests some of the duties and starts the reader thinking: "How do I do this? Maybe I do need some training." Finally, give another biblical basis for how to operate in the ministry.

Remember, some people may have never read a job description in a church. Make it simple but complete so everyone knows the definition of a good job. The introduction should just be enough to give the people a little overview, but do not go into a lot of detail about job performance.

JOB DUTIES

These are examples. You must tailor yours to the church plant you occupy and cover only what the usher does. In a small church, they may do almost everything; in a larger church they will be more specialized and even have numbered positions.

- Ushers should arrive *x* minutes early, with head usher arriving ten minutes before the others.
- Make sure the church is clean and tidy, including bathrooms.
- Set up chairs correctly.
- Police the parking lot, entry, and sidewalks.
- The A/C or heat should properly adjusted.
- The proper doors should unlocked (or locked).

(The above items may be handled by janitorial staff (if you have one). In small churches, the users do it.

- Overhead projector readied unless, you have an audio visual ministry.
- Offer containers positioned for use with envelopes and visitor information close at hand.
- Water and cups placed for pulpit and musicians. Tissues and anointing oil at or near the altar area.
- Covers or drop cloths available for female altar attendants and ushers.
- Be dresses and groomed to the standard of the church. Some may have badges or special coats for ushers so they can be identified.

(Here, let us remember other ministries with special dress needs. Women in the nursery or with little children must wear pants, not dresses or skirts. They may have to assume unflattering positions to ride herd on the kids, and we do not want any embarrassments.)

- Clean shaven or neat beards. Take a vacation from your duties while you cultivate your beard!
- Clean of body and breath. Have breath mints on your person. Use deodorant or good-smelling liquids if you have a body odor problem. We talk about this here so we don't have to mention it later.
- Health: If you have the sniffles or another attack of the enemy that might offend or be contagious, call your supervisor and do not serve that week. This is especially important when working with children.

As you add to your list, let your imagination run wild. The first copy is for you alone, so put everything you can conjure up down on paper. Remember that you may have a new person to church who knows nothing about the technicalities of working in your ministry. You can always edit, but don't forget anything important. Here are more items to consider.

- Know where all facilities are located. Little maps can be duplicated so each usher has one. When someone asks directions of an usher, it is not a good thing to reply, "I don't know."
- Following the above, a list of all church leaders, the council, and leadership should be made up and given to each usher so he or she can point out the correct person when asked, and can advise correctly when a ministry opportunity turns up in the area.
- Make an effort to seat folks in the front seats first so the latecomers do not disrupt the service. Some churches block off the last two rows until the song service is half over.
- Opening Prayer: Sometime after everyone arrives and prior to the start of their duties, the head usher should gather the workers, and perhaps the music people, and pray for the pastor and for needs to be met during the service. Then while you are at your position, intercede in the Spirit when you are not actually doing a task.
- This is something that should be done by all workers at all ministries, especially praying over the children. Ushers should pray in tongues while standing behind someone in a prayer line (catching people if they fall).
- Maintain decency and order in love. During the gifts of the Spirit, prohibit entry and movement in the service as best you can without being too obvious.
- Pray for crying children, inattentive teens, and full bladders so distractions due to noise and movement are minimized.
- Be ready at all times to cast out demons, lay hands on the sick so they may be healed, and salvation and baptism in the Holy Spirit.
- Work inconspicuously; people are supposed to have their attention on the giving of the Word, not the workers. Be as invisible as possible.

Here, you future leaders should take note. Some enter Helps to get noticed. They my see this as their opportunity to "be somebody." Experience has shown that the best church workers do it as worship to the Lord, not as a way to aggrandize themselves. Be aware, and if you see the tendency in one of your workers to have a "look at me" attitude, nip it in the bud.

- The head usher is usually in charge of the sanctuary when the pastor is in the pulpit. Emergency messages or needs or gifts of the Holy Spirit for the edification of the church should be presented to the head usher. Don't let people walk up to the platform.
- The pastor and head usher should have prearranged nonverbal signals for use during the service.
- During services, the head usher leads all ministries. He can direct the activities of any worker. Before and after service, the normal organizational table applies.

Head ushers must be sensitive to the other leaders and let them lead their people whenever possible.

• Sometimes ushers will be separated from their families during a service. Rotate them so it happens as little as possible. When you are with family, do not hold babies. You must be able to act immediately.

• Keep your eyes open, even when the pastor says "all eyes closed." You must be able to spot people fidgeting or raising their hands slightly, and point them out to the exhorters or a pastor later. Also, you must guard the assembly from someone who would disrupt during an altar call. You can get into the Spirit when you are not needed on your job. That is what rotation is all about.

A word here: As leaders, we must adequately man each ministry so there is backup and extras so no one gets burned out. It is better to go without a ministry than to do it with an inadequate number of people and have it fall apart because everyone gets used too much. This is part of the planning process. How many people do you need to man your ministry so no one gets used too much?

• Offerings. Take your cue from the people in the pulpit. They may want the ushers to clap and stomp in joy at the mention of an offering, or they may want it more dignified. Some pass the bucket or plate; some may have the congregation bring their tithes and offerings up front. This is a local option, but it needs to be clear to both ushers and congregation.

• Counting of the offering. *Always have two people count.* Rotate the people so the same two do not always serve together. This prevents ushers from getting too familiar with who is giving and who is not. Also, switching pairs reduces the possibility that the tempter can enter into the process and steal. The head usher should rotate through this detail along with the other ushers and church leaders.

• Any time you have a ministry with valuable property or money, you must have adequate safeguards in place. We are stewards of God's property and must take it seriously.

• Assisting in communion. A set procedure must be developed: who comes in early and sets up, who cleans up, and which usher serves those on the platform, the audio visual, and the children's church. Lay it out item by item so there is a clear picture of who does what. Confusion must not occur during a service.

• Altar calls. This is a specialized part of ushering that is not done everywhere. In major ministries and many prominent evangelist ministries, we see large altar calls with many users acting as directors and catchers. In the local church, it happens less often. However, wise planning suggests that having a written plan in effect, and training in operating during an altar call, is essential if it is to go smoothly.

SOME ADDITIONAL TIPS AND SUGGESTIONS FOR YOUR OUTLINE

- When you have guest ministers, the head usher should talk with them and get their preferences for altar calls and other changes in the order of a service. If they have none, explain yours and get their agreement not to change things in the middle of the service.

- Keep lines in order. Lines should be only one person deep so that catchers can move freely behind them. People waiting should be kept in the aisles and queued up front as space permits.

- Let no one touch the person being prayed for except the minister in charge. Ministers will ask if they want help. Pray in tongues (quietly) behind them and watch (and listen to) the preacher and the person you are behind.

- Catchers hold at the elbow and small of the back, not the armpits. Armpit catching can ruin the back and your reputation if your hands go around the front of a female.

- A female usher should always be present and instantly place a drop cloth over females, preferably on the way down. This takes grace and finesse, but with practice it is easily done.

- Have ushers in the rear to control movement and noise.

- Unless the service has been dismissed from the pulpit, folks should be encouraged to stay in their seats and pray.

- Again, ushers do not close their eyes and bow their heads during altar calls unless they are in the front seats, and then they should bow but keep their eyes open. It is important to be able to identify timid folks who fidget or partially raise their hands, and to have someone lovingly inquire if they need prayer. Ushers point them out to the exhorters or prayer team for follow-up.

- Ushers positions should be numbered, and separate job outlines should be made for each position. For example, number 1 is the primary catcher and sits up front, and number 2 sits on the other side in the front. They are responsible for keeping order on the platform and are the primary men catching. A female usher or other designated female should also be in front for covering duties. Then number 3, number 4, and higher numbers are given the farther back in the sanctuary they go.

- The head usher will usually stay in the back until the altar call and then move to the front to queue people into the prayer line and supervise the ushers in front. The head usher will also read signals from the pastor or pulpit minister and advise the prayer team about the need of the person so that after the altar call, they can follow up and give encouragement, or a tract or a Bible if it is a salvation.

- Outside and parking lot duties are where ushers rotate so they can be with their families during service. Outside ushers have no duties during service, so they are free to get in the Spirit, participate fully in worship, and not be bothered about any potential for duties.

Again, I must emphasize this. There must be depth in ministry. We cannot have the same people doing the same thing all the time; this can cause people to feel used. Also they cannot be ministered to if they are always ministering.

This outline is for training, and it is purposely very detailed. In your outline, cover:

- *What has to be done*
- *Who will be doing it*
- *How will you do it*

Giving workers an outline lets them know the definition of a good job. They have something to which they can aspire. Fear that the job is too complicated, or that they have no experience, prevents some from participating. Explain that you have outlines and will give training. Once they believe they can do it, they can.

When you make your list of things, arrange it in order of what has to be done and down to what would be nice to have done. In other words, list the things that are inflexible (like being saved and baptized in the Holy Spirit, being on time, showing up when you promise to) first, and then go down in importance to the preference items.

To review:

- *First the title page with the two or three paragraphs of description of the ministry and what it accomplishes*
- *Next the list of the duties, with the mandatory first down to the preference items.*
- *In some ministries, there may be monetary considerations. They must be addressed separately, though not in the job description. They must be addressed so the leadership can make judgments on whether there are sufficient resources for all the needs of the church.*

END OF LESSON. HALLELUJAH!

Your pastor will present your certificate of completion at a church service soon.

God bless you all, and may God get all the glory for the good work you do.